My Bes␣ ␣␣␣␣

Letters To...
Our Teenage Daughters

By
Michael Kenneth Chapman

Edited by
Two Time Emmy Nominee
Margaret Ford-Taylor

My Best Advice
Letters To…
***Our* Teenage Daughters**

Michael K. Chapman
Co-Author

DEDICATION

I dedicate this book…

…To my wonderful mother Pastor Eloise C. Corbin, for always encouraging me and teaching me the importance of faith and the power of prayer. Thanks **"momma"** for all the sacrifices you have made so I can live my dreams. With all my heart…I love you!

…In loving memory of my *"Big sister"*
Debra Marie Chapman…You will always be missed.

How To Use This Empowerment Tool Book:

1st. **READ** your daily empowerment letter based on the *date* of your current calendar.

2nd. **W R I T E** in your journal a new thought or idea immediately. Also, read page 143 on how to set and achieve your goals.

3rd. **SPEAK** out loud your **"I-Promise"** affirmations twice daily (morning & afternoon) see page 4.

ENJOY! ENJOY! ENJOY!

This Book Is
Exclusively For

_____

From: _____

_____

_____

_____

_____

"I Promise"

- **I promise** I will not make EXCUSES...but make adjustments.

- **I promise** I will **RESPECT** myself, my peers, my teachers and all adults in and out of school.

- **I promise** I will be prepared for school every day because that is **MY RESPONSIBILITY**.

- **I promise** I will complete all my school assignments on time and *seek assistance immediately* as I need it.

- **I promise** I will go to school **EVERY DAY** and maintain a positive attitude...ALL DAY.

- **I promise** I will **VALUE my EDUCATION** by placing it so HIGH that nothing comes before it...**ABSOLUTELY NOTHING!**

- **I promise** I will read this DECLARATION AND MY GOALS twice a day!

- **I promise** I will say to myself, *"If I fail at any or all of these endeavors, I will forgive myself and try even harder tomorrow!"*

INTRODUCTION

Introduction. I read where billionaire entrepreneur Oprah Winfrey once said *"even the wildest dreams have to start somewhere. Allow yourself the time and space to let your mind wonder and your imagination to fly."* With that said, you hold in your hands a book that was written from an idea, but mostly from the heart and souls of 31 successful women from the U.S. and the U.K. From the onset I must inform you that this book is not intended as a one-stop to solve all your life's issues. However, if you wish to change your life for the better, build stronger relationships, learn to set and achieve your goals, learn some new skills and new ideas about self-respect, self-esteem and self-confidence, then, in your hands, you have a road map, a blue print that will help you to BEGIN to structure or restructure your life and your future. An ancient African Proverb says…*"It takes a village to raise a child."* Consider this book the collective thoughts and advice gathered from within that village. This empowerment tool book has been thoughtfully put together with young women in mind, because we know we are obligated to do everything in our power to ensure that our daughters (and sons) become vibrant and contributing members of society. Let me share a story that demonstrates the power of an idea coupled with persistence. It concerns the birth and creation of this book.

Inception. From the time my God-daughter Mariah Weaver (whom I affectionately call ***"Precious"***) was 14 years of age I would hand write and mail her an encouragement letter every other month. Though she lives less than 10 miles away I thought it was "cool" for her to receive a letter in the mail in the midst of all the bills and junk mail mom was receiving. My purpose was to encourage her to do well in school; *i.e.* to respect herself, her peers and adults, and to *place a high value* on her education so that nothing could touch it. I was keenly aware that the second half of her sophomore year she would be facing the infamous five-part Ohio Graduation Test (OGT). Before testing time came I restructured the letters with a new purpose in mind because I wanted to do all I could to increase herself-confidence for the test. One of the methods I initiated was the power of "self-talk." I designed a declaration entitled ***"I-Promise"*** and she was to read it aloud in the morning, before lunch and before bed time. There is one included in this book as well (see page 4) and just as powerful. OGT testing time came and by the grace of God, tutoring, and hard work Mariah, passed all five parts on her first try. Two years quickly went by and she was a senior set to graduate in June of 2010 from Shaw High School in East Cleveland, Ohio. One day, as I was giving some thought to a creative graduation gift, I had what I considered to be an ingenious idea!

The Power of an Idea. That idea was to petition 31-women to write a letter about the ups and downs of life after high school. I would get the letters edited, put them in a binder, title it and present it to my Goddaughter as a book entitled, *"My Best Advice: Letters To...My Graduating Daughter."* Unfortunately time ran out. Cash is always a

Good trump-card, so I played my hand and made a cash gift at graduation time instead. However, the idea of 31-letters in book form never died. In early August of the same year, and after conversations with several friends I decided to take on the challenge of putting my idea into book form. The first thing I did was to research teen topics and issues and that is how I chose the 12-hot topics found in this book. Next, I asked 31 women to pick a topic to write about.

Finally, I pitched my idea to Miss Ford-Taylor (see About Editor), to see if she would edit the 31 letters. Unequivocally, she said YES!

Finally. From August 2010 through May 2012 I worked diligently to complete this book project. The journey was interesting to say the least. I can recall several times when I almost threw in the towel even though I believed passionately in the project and what I was doing. My intent was to keep my goals in front of me and not to lose focus. I admit I was driven. As a matter of fact, some people became a little annoyed because all I would talk about was "the book." I remember one particularly discouraging period when the project stalled as I waited for responses from contributors. At first, I panicked. And then I got angry. I knew this was a wonderful, worthwhile project. Why wasn't it moving? Finally, I stood flat-footed in front of the mirror with tears streaming down my face and said "Michael, come hell or high water you're not quitting no matter what happens or how long it takes." I told myself that *"greater is He who is in me than he who is in the world."* By the way, I had to visit the mirror several times on the journey, but I was determined not to quit.

To be honest, I had dropped the ball other times in my past and this time I was committed to go all the way. Plus, something inside would not let me quit. Shortly after the first "reckoning," I received an e-mail with a letter attached to it. The following month I received another e-mail and it was a powerful letter as well. Then the thought came to me, what better way was there of getting in touch with and engaging dynamic, caring women who would keep the ball rolling than through women who had those same traits? So to keep the momentum going, I asked the selected women not only to contribute but also for as many referrals as they could give me. As you can see, it worked. The evidence is in your hands. So, read, read, read, use and enjoy. I sincerely believe there is something life-giving in this book for everyone.

Michael K. Chapman
Co-Author

CONTENTS

Part One

31-Empowerment Letters & Journal

Part Two

"What a lot we lost when we stopped writing letters. You can't re-read a phone call."

-Liz Carpenter

PART ONE

31-EMPOWERMENT LETTERS

&

PRIVATE JOURNAL

EMPOWERMENT DAY 1

By Annette Odom

SELF-ESTEEM

Dear Sweetheart,

My best advice for you today relates to self-esteem. Due to mass media, teenage girls are inundated with images of what is portrayed as beautiful; that is a very thin, almost anorexic looking female, usually with straight hair past her shoulders with a complexion that barely contains melanin and wearing the latest designer clothing. Honey, look around you and you will know that this is false. You will see many wonderful and beautiful females who do not fit this image. You will also begin to realize that this stereotypical outside image has nothing at all to do with what and who a person really is. Let's take a poll. How many female judges will you find that fit this image? How many lawyers? How many doctors? How many business women? How many scientists or world leaders? How many educators or political figures? Investigate all careers and you will find that the only one that requires you to be thin is modeling and NOT ONE is based on skin color.

As for hair, there are as many varieties of length, texture, style and color as there are people to imagine them. If you take your research a little further you will find that most women who do hold successful, prominent positions are surrounded by people who love and appreciate them. And even though their place in society gives them a healthy sense of self-worth, they know that their outside appearance does not necessarily define them and that it is only the beginning. How did they get this sense of self- worth? Well, they first appreciated themselves. At some point, they took a good look at themselves and said, "This is good." Sweetheart, can you do that? Try it. Stand before a full length mirror, take a good look at yourself and say, "This is good." Say it until you mean it. If you have a weight problem, sit down and make a plan for fewer calories and more exercise and stick to it. If you have a skin problem, sit down and make a plan to drink more water, cut out sweets and greasy foods and deep clean your face more often. In other words, most legitimate criticisms that you might have of your appearance can be addressed and will also help you gain and maintain good health in the bargain. But never, ever criticize yourself based upon some image that is not you. Choose hair styles that fit YOU. Buy clothes that flatter YOU. You have been given EVERYTHING to make YOU beautiful. You can be under five feet or over six feet, thin as a rail or a full figured wonder or anything in between. Your skin coloring can be yellow, red, jet black to caramel brown to oyster white or any combination. God saw what you were to be and said, "This is good." Now, it's your turn to appreciate that unique one-of-a-kind you. When you stop worrying about looking like everybody else or like somebody you saw in a magazine or a video you will know you have begun to be your own person and that's when you'll be able to stand before the mirror with confident self-esteem, throw your shoulders back and with a great big smile honestly and truthfully say, "THIS IS GOOD." Next stop? THE WORLD!

Love Always

DAY 1 JOURNAL

_____

_____

_____

_____

_____

_____

_____

_____

_____

_____

_____

_____

_____

_____

_____

_____

_____

_____

_____

_____

EMPOWERMENT DAY 2

By Latoya Renee Walton

DATING

Dear Sweet heart,

My best advice for you today regarding dating on this wonderful, beautiful day is; **FIRST**, think about why you want to date and then who you should date. As a teen, you're often told what to do and what not to do, what to wear, how to act, or who not to date. Today, let's focus on what you should do for yourself. Ready? First make a list of standards. It is important to set standards BEFORE you get caught up emotionally which may distract your judgment. Your list of standards will reflect the characteristics you want and like in a guy. They should include the spiritual, the emotional, the intellectual and the physical. I place physical last because, too often, girls look at the physical side of a boy only which is a big, big mistake. The physical is only what you can see on the outside. It often has very little to do with what's going on inside a person's head. The guy that you might have the most fun dating may not be your physical ideal at all.

Don't cheat yourself by dating someone simply for his looks. Another important lookout point is this. You are of an age when many physical changes are occurring with your body. Your physical response to the opposite sex becomes stronger and stronger. It's natural. It's normal. But be careful not to let these physical responses be your guide in dating. Teen dating is a time to have fun! A time to get to know yourself and others. Save the heavy stuff until after you have completed your education and you're ready to begin that part of your life as a mature, responsible adult. Right now, ENJOY being a teen. It will never happen again.

Finally, check and recheck your list, OFTEN. As you mature in the dating process your list may expand or become more detailed. It should never shrink and you should never settle for less than what is best for you. The person that you date should want that too. God bless and keep you sweetheart.

Love Always

DAY 2 JOURNAL

EMPOWERMENT DAY 3

By Anonymous

PEER-PRESSURE

Dear Sweetheart,

My best advice for you today is about peer-pressure. This is a story, mostly about me, but one that I think has important lessons for anyone but especially for my most prized gift-YOU! The subject reminds me of a 1980's movie entitled *"Some Kind of Wonderful"* about a popular girl and a not-so-popular boy. In one conversation the girl states, "I'd rather be with someone for the wrong reason than to be alone for the right reason." The boy tops it by saying, "I'd rather be right." I thought about this conversation many time during my high school and college years. It made me wonder why I couldn't be strong enough to stand on my own two feet and shun the "untrue friends." You see, I measured the relationships I had by the quantity of years I was friends with a person, not by the quality of the relationship. It didn't matter if I was called names and teased because as long as I had people to sit with at lunch and hang out with on the weekends, I accepted how I was treated. I didn't realize I had a choice.

Oh how I wish I had known! How I wish I had reflected on how battered my self-esteem was from associating with those people. When did I figure this out? Way too late for my teen years. It was when I took a course after graduate school on bullying and realized that I was the target of relational aggression. Look it up. It's important. "Relational Aggression." I came to the realization that these "friends" were really bullies and that I was too afraid to stand up for myself. The end result was a battered self-esteem from wanting to fit in and belong. The saddest part is, I can look back now and know that I had a choice. I can't do anything about the past but what I can do today is tell you, with all the love and passion that is in me, SWEETHEART, YOU HAVE A CHOICE, TOO! Think of the mantra: "Treat others the way you would like to be treated." If the friendship or relationship does not make you feel good about yourself, GET OUT! There are other people who will be your friend and whom you can befriend. If you're in a relationship that makes you feel uncomfortable, talk to someone you trust. Certain adults can be your best ally. Develop a new hobby. Join something new such as a sports club or art class or take up an instrument. Think outside of" your circle." Look outside of your school, even. There are kids your age with similar interests who might not go to your school.

Look at youth groups, your church, synagogue, or mosque. Reinvent your image of you. Put people in your life who appreciate you because you deserve to be appreciated as you are. Indecisions small or large and regardless of the pressure remember first and always, BE TRUE TO YOURSELF.

Love Always

DAY 3 JOURNAL

EMPOWERMENT DAY 4

By Rebecca Rubio

RELATIONSHIPS

Dear Sweetheart,

My best advice for you today regarding relationships is this: Take inventory of self. It is not easy but it is important that your heart and head form an honest and healthy relationship. That outside that you look at in the mirror every day is only part of you and no matter what you see, it is not the most important part. You will want to take the best of your inside self, the part that no one sees or knows about but you, and find a balance for the two. Know yourself inside and out because if you don't, others will begin to define who you are simply by what they see on the outside. Become your own best friend and strengthen all those good inside things and qualities. Learn to love your whole God-given self. After yourself, your next critical relationship is with your parents. Please do not expect us to be perfect. We can only do the best that we can with what we have. We can only do what we know how to do and every human being living makes mistakes. We are no exception.

Actually, there may be many mistakes but now that you are A teenager; it is time to forge a new kind of relationship with your parents. In the new relationship you will help your parents to continue to help you. In your growing maturity, you will forgive their mistakes because you know that they love you and have your best interest at heart. In this new relationship you will ask questions about things that confuse you or that you don't understand and you will be willing to listen openly to what your parents have to say for the same reasons.

Strive hard, my dear, not to let offenses, anger, disappointments or misunderstandings divide you from your parents *because* _you are a unit and there is power in unity_. The unit includes the whole family so embrace this group God has placed around you. Listen to them, learn from the mistakes of older members and be there as a part of the support system for younger ones. Teach them what you have been taught. Try to love them all, unconditionally. Using this solid relationship with self and family as your guide and inspiration, enjoy your life and move forward in to new relationships and toward maturity with pride and confidence.

Love Always

DAY 4 JOURNAL

_____

_____

_____

_____

_____

_____

_____

_____

_____

_____

_____

_____

_____

_____

_____

_____

_____

_____

_____

_____

_____

_____

_____

_____

_____

_____

EMPOWERMENT DAY 5

By Cynthia Grant

ABUSE

Dear Sweetheart,

My best advice for you today deals with abuse: physical, mental, emotional and spiritual.

First, know the signs. Often, abuse begins subtly and builds so slowly the abused party isn't even aware of it until it has become a way of life. They often begin to believe that this kind of relationship is "normal" or the kind of treatment they deserve. WRONG! Know the signs. Any treatment, action or language that limits, restricts, discourages growth and the use and development of God-given talents and skills or makes you feel "less than" in any way, is abuse. Repeat: Any treatment, action or language that limits, restricts, discourages growth and the use and development of God-given talents and skills or makes you feel "less than" in any way, is abuse. It is a form of hatred in disguise. Next, know that you do not deserve anything but the best that this life has to offer. Determine that you will not accept less because you do not have to. Ever.

Anyone who offers you less is the enemy. There is no room for compromise. Next, nip it in the bud, that is, STOP IT! IMMEDIATELY! Let the person know how you feel. If you have a loving caring relationship, the other person will want to know if they are making you feel less than you should. On the other hand, if the other person finds so much wrong with you that they have to correct you or change you, there is a problem and the problem is not you, it's the relationship. Don't argue about it, just know that that person should go and find someone who suits their needs and you should wait for someone who can appreciate you for the wonderful, beautiful, sharing, caring person you are. Believe me, they are looking for you. Honey, in a healthy male/female relationship, neither party should be looking for a parent or a child to boss around, mold, raise or correct. The relationship should be based upon mutual love, respect and appreciation of who the other partner already is and what they bring to complete the union.

Next, TELL! No matter who it is, no matter what the relationship. If you suspect abuse you probably are being abused. Also, if a partner physically abuses you once, they will do it again. TELL! Abusers thrive in secrecy and abuse cannot stand the shining light of truth and honesty. No matter what disguise it comes in, it's a coward's tool.

Avoid isolation and Tell! Let friends and loved ones be there for you. Finally, continue to love yourself. It's the best defense a person can have against someone else's attempted abuse. We protect what we love!

Love Always

DAY 5 JOURNAL

EMPOWERMENT DAY 6

By Miracle LaSeane Reid

LOVE

Dear Sweetheart,

My best advice for you today regarding love is, when you love; your feelings of affection are intense, strong and undeniable. I am sure you can best relate to the feeling of love when you think of God, your parents, siblings, extended family members, close friends and may be even your pets. You might even experience feelings of love when you are about to travel to a particular place that you are fond of or when you eat one of your favorite foods, engage in your favorite hobby or listen to your favorite artist or song. Whoever or whatever you love, you do it with your whole heart and you experience joy in the process.

There will also come a time in your life when you will experience love of a romantic nature. Romantic love may leave you breathless. It can sometimes cause your palms to sweat, your heart may race and your thoughts may constantly be about this individual.

You may even experience an unexplainable feeling of joy and excitement when you know you are going to see this person or are with this person. Romantic love can be beautiful when both parties share mutual feelings and have a mutual respect for one another. Now, you may be the kind of person who loves more easily, have stronger feelings or make more of a commitment to a blossoming relationship than your young man. That is why you must first learn to love yourself. Loving yourself will help you avoid some of the pitfalls that you may encounter such as the pressure of feeling the need to be physical with someone before you are ready or before you should. For example, you are not obligated to have sex with a young man just because he says he loves you. As a matter of fact, if he really loves you, he will understand that teenage sex is not in your best interest. Physical love, or sex, should be the final step in a **marriage** relationship. Not an experiment in love. Whatever the case, never do anything so that you don't have regrets. Remember, once you do an act, there is no **"undo"** button. Not only should you be careful about sharing your physical body but also be careful not to subject yourself to any verbal, emotional or physical abuse.

If a young man loves you and respects you, he will never be little you, call you out of your name or pressure you into doing unnecessary and/or uncomfortable acts. There is never a justifiable reason why a boyfriend should put his hands on you. If you allow any of these forms of abuse to happen, BEWARE! This is evidence of low self-esteem and opens the door for cycles like these to repeat themselves over and over. Ask yourself, if I really love myself, would I allow someone to treat me badly? The answer, of course, is NO!

Sweetheart, you are precious to God, your parents, siblings, extended family and friends. All or some of these individuals have shown you love in some way at one time or another in their words or actions. Because of them, you have good examples of love to follow. Please realize that you deserve only the best that life has to offer and when you love yourself as they love you, the best is all you will accept.

Love Always

DAY 6 JOURNAL

_____

_____

_____

_____

_____

_____

_____

_____

_____

_____

_____

_____

_____

_____

_____

_____

_____

_____

_____

_____

_____

_____

EMPOWERMENT DAY 7

By Anonymous

SEX vs. ABSTINENCE

Dear Sweetheart,

My best advice for you today concerns sex versus abstinence. Most of us adults can think back and wish we could change some mistake we made in the past. We can't. My darling girl, there are consequences for every action and the time to think about those consequences is **BEFORE you act**. The best way to avoid the consequences of having sex is to abstain from having sex until you are a **MARRIED ADULT**. I advise that because no matter how hard it may become decide **NOW** TO CHOOSE ABSTINENCE. Make this very important decision NOW! I PROMISE YOU, you will never ever regret it. Decide that **ABSTINENCE** will be **YOUR CHOICE!** My grandmother used to advise me not to have sex as a teenager. She used to say, *"Why buy a cow when you can get free milk?"* Well, I couldn't wait. So I had my son, who is now fourteen, when I was fifteen years old. I love him with all of my being BUT if I could do it all over again, I would have waited.

I was fortunate not to have been exposed to any Sexually Transmitted Diseases. His father and I did not get married and he is no longer a part of my life. I found that sex before you are a married adult is a huge distraction from what you ought to be doing which is **PREPARING** for adulthood. You look at your maturing body. It looks grown up. You have all of these grown up feelings. The media tells you, you're grown up. Trust me, Sweetheart, they are deceiving. Can you vote? No, because you're not really grown up. Can you sign a legally binding contract? No, because you're really not grown up. The list goes on but the point is sex should be for **MARRIED ADULTS ONLY**. Just because you can does not mean that you should. Having teenage sex puts you on an emotional roller coaster that moves everything else, your school work, your family and friends, everything, to the back ground. At this stage of your life, **having sex will STOP** you from being the best person you can be. Don't get me wrong. Sexual feelings are a natural part of growing up. They will continue for the rest of your life. Try not to become a victim of your own feelings, thoughts and emotions.

The Secret? Let me give you some practical advice that you can actually use. **<u>STAY ACTIVE!</u>** Lots of physical exercise and cold baths do work! Keep your mind filled and your schedule busy with your studies, hobbies and the business of growing up. ***Don't be ashamed of your feelings and curiosity. They're natural.*** Discuss them with a friend or, then go run around the track a few times to get your mind and body headed in another direction away from sexual experimentation. Find another physical outlet. Something else—boys and men will ALWAYS be there but the right man, the responsible, committed, adult man--the one you want to build a life with will appreciate the fact that you had enough COURAGE, enough SELF-RESPECT, and enough SENSE to wait-for him.

Love Always

DAY 7 JOURNAL

_____

_____

_____

_____

_____

_____

_____

_____

_____

_____

_____

_____

_____

_____

_____

_____

_____

_____

_____

_____

_____

_____

_____

_____

_____

EMPOWERMENT DAY 8

By Liz Hagan Kanche

RELATIONSHIPS

Dear Sweetheart,

my best advice for you today is about relationships. Having been both, I know relationships with adults can be tough when you're a teenager. It becomes hard to impossible for adults to recall all of those new feelings, those fears, hopes and dreams they experienced as a teenager and because the teen is just entering that phase of his or her own life and has no reference point that is, does not know their parent's whole story-it becomes a challenge for both to understand each other's perspective. That's why I am so happy that we are taking this opportunity to share and communicate on this very important aspect of everyone's life. I LOVE YOU and that's the bottom line. Hope fully, you will take what you can from what I give and use it to build upon. What you think you cannot use, just gently tuck away until another time, okay? First, let me share with you that living is not a passive experience. Your growth, what you do with your life, the relationships you have, each constitutes an <u>active</u> experience. Therefore, since it's your life, you must be an <u>active</u> participant. In other words, try not to let things "just happen" to you or for you. As long as you live, you will be in some sort of relationship with someone, beginning with your family. Now, your family is your family, true, but <u>you</u> go a long way in determining what kind of relationship you will have even with them. What positive thing, act, words do <u>you</u> bring to the relationship? What positive things do <u>you</u> do or say to help each situation? You can ask the same questions when it comes to teachers and other adults in your life. So, since your relationship with others will always be at the center of your life, setting a few ground rules for yourself now is one of the smartest things you can do. Actually, it's time to start taking notes about the kind of person or adult you want and plan to be, period. Each time you will discover that it is all tied into your relationship with others. My first specific advice to you is always, always, be yourself. That is, stay true to yourself but remember you can learn something from everyone you come in contact with even if it is a negative you want to avoid in the future. Hopefully, you will continue to learn all of your life but right now learning is your main job. Try to see yourself as a student—not just of science and math and the other subjects you have at school but of life.

Keep a daily journal about feelings and relationships. You may be surprised at how fast feelings, friends and circumstances can change or shift. A most important part of this exercise is to record what you learn from each experience. This is also an opportunity for you to have a record for the future that can be referred to when it's your time to raise a child or lead a classroom.

Next, take advantage of positive opportunities. Since our friends are such an important part of our lives, friendship is a relationship that we should examine often. We should always consider how we feel and act when we are with those friends. If it isn't the way you want to feel or act, sorry, but you are not with the right people for you. Never be afraid to stand up for what you believe. Don't just follow the crowd. The right people for you are there, all around you so be careful about judging people just because they don't look, talk, or live the way you do. Begin to look beyond the surface. They could be the right kind of people for you to learn from, grow from, have a meaningful relationship with. What do you like to door wish you could do? Try joining a sports team or some other after school activity that might interest you. If the first one doesn't work, don't give up. Try another one. Visit a place of worship that has young people. Keep on until you find the right people for you and you'll find yourself in the right kind of relationships. Be active in the decision to surround yourself with positive people doing positive things.

Finally, in relationships of the heart, by all means live, have fun and enjoy but make a decision to save intimate, one on one relationships for a later period in your life. If there is a decision to be made, make your first response NO. Any relationship that is worth YOU will still be there when you have given it thought. Next, ask yourself, "Will this person be there with me, for me, through the rest of high school, college, jobs, trips around the country, the world? Do I want them to be? What kind of person will we both be when we finish growing up?" Ask yourself these critical questions, consider the many examples all around you and then WAIT! You'll be so glad you did. YOU are a great gift to give your future lifelong partner. My love, the world is fast and loud. Step out of it and listen from time to time. You'll be surprised and over joyed at the kind of life and relationships that are waiting for you and only you.

Love Always

DAY 8 JOURNAL

EMPOWERMENT DAY 9

By Katrina L. McKenzie

SELF-ESTEEM

Dear Sweetheart,

My best advice for you today is about self-esteem. On this wonderful and glorious day I say to you, embrace the young woman you see in the mirror. She is very special. Take the time to know her, physically, mentally and emotionally. Take inventory and become acquainted with her. She is, or should be, your very best friend. First, let's look at the physical. What do you see? Are you pleased? You should be. It is a unique face. Everything about it is a story waiting to be told, a story going back generations and generations. You are the result of so many people who lived before you. In your face, you carry the results of their joys and sorrows, their triumphs and tragedies. Even the pimple has a story to tell and the scar has taken a journey. Your eyes hold secrets of whom and what you are, where you've been and where you're going. Your lips speak victory, peace pain, joy and triumph. Your hair, kinky, curly or straight has its own special relative power.

Mentally, the person in the mirror has the power to learn, to store, use, record and disseminate information to advance herself and influence her world. Emotionally, she is a gold mine of feelings and fantasies; a store-house of the kinds of dreams that have sheltered and advanced civilizations since the beginning of time.

That's your reflection in the mirror. Embrace it. Embrace the self-esteem that it embodies. More than that embrace the power that comes from that self-esteem. It belongs to you.

Love Always

DAY 9 JOURNAL

EMPOWERMENT DAY 10

By Shiryl A. Chambers

LOVE

Dear Sweetheart,

My best advice for you today concerns Love. What is love? Well, it is the strongest positive emotion you can feel. Love is caring, sharing, and giving. Love is respect. Love is patient, not demanding and love is unconditional. Love does not require you to **"prove"** anything. You don't have to prove anything to keep your parent's love and you don't have to "prove" anything to keep God's love. All other professions of love should be based on these two examples. Friends, male and female, will love you for you if they are truly friends. And that brings us to the most important question of the day. Do you love you? Are you satisfied with who and what you are? Are you **kind**? **Considerate? Respectful? Compassionate? Loyal? Clean? Honest? Helpful? Responsible?** Are you working to keep a balance in your life between your appearance, school work, family, friends, health, and recreational activities and, of course, shopping? Yes, there's a lot to consider but that's what growing up is all about and these are the attributes that will complete you and make you a lovable person. Honey, please get out a pencil and a piece of paper and finish the list. First, write down all of the positive qualities you know about yourself and you'll find that you're a pretty special person already. Next, what are some of the things you want or need to work on to help you finish becoming the kind of person you want to be? Write them down and then work on them daily. You'll find as you work on yourself, your vision of whom and what you are will grow. Self-confidence will grow with self-respect. Your standards and expectations will shift and expand. You will begin to expect and to know that you deserve the best that love has to offer from anyone who enters your life. They will know it, too. In the meantime, enjoy your youth, Sweetheart and always, always remember, love YOU first!

Love Always

DAY 10 JOURNAL

EMPOWERMENT DAY 11

By Teresa L. Conley

BULLYING

Dear Sweetheart,

My best advice to you today is about bullying. The first most important thing you have to know about a bully is that you are actually the stronger of the two. That's right. It doesn't matter if the bully is physically stronger than you, it doesn't matter how they look or how smart they think they are. All bullies have one thing in common. They are all miserable, insecure cowards. The situation may change but that fact does not. Honey, a bully can only bully you if you feel you deserve to be bullied. Did you know that? Also, if you feel like that, somehow you don't know your own worth. I know you are worth the world. So, the first thing I want you to do is to get in a quiet space, alone, and say this, "From the beginning of time until the end of time, no one has ever looked or felt exactly like me. Therefore, I am **unique** and **wonderful** and **special**. I deserve only the best including the best treatment. Knowing this, I will always hold my head up high and appreciate who and what I am while always striving to be the best me that I can be. No one has the right to try and take that away from me and I will never let them." If you make this your daily motto, your mantra, and believe it no one will ever bully you because you won't let them. Now, there are many forms of bullying.

Teasing that hurts and sexual remarks from the opposite sex, regardless of age, are always of bullying. How do you know? I fit makes you feel uncomfortable, it's an attempt to bully you. If someone is constantly putting you down and making you feel bad about yourself, that's bullying. Whatever the case, repeat the phrase above several times and then tell that person to go get a life because you are in charge of yours. If it's an adult or authority figure and you can't say it out loud, *you can think it.* Don't let yourself droop into self-pity, uncertainty and confusion. Say to yourself, "I know I am finding my way but I also know that I am worthy and therefore I will find it." And you will. Spreading private information, pictures and lies by internet has become another popular bullying tool. Stay strong. Hold your head high. The people who love you will continue to love, respect and trust you. Let us help you. We are bigger than the problem.

The others truly do not matter. Just don't keep it to yourself. Internet bullying is illegal. The person can be prosecuted. **TELL** your parents or the school counselor. The only way the bully can win is if you keep it to yourself. On the physical side, the second someone touches you, they have broken the law. Don't be quiet. The bully has a problem and it's not yours.

TELL. **TELL** your parents. **TELL** your teachers. **TELL** your friends. **TELL** any adult you trust. Don't be afraid to go to the authorities. The important thing is-**TELL**. If it's a boyfriend, he's no friend. No matter how small the gesture, no one has the right to touch you without your permission. Another scenario is this, because they are cowards, bullies often surround themselves with groups of people who are weaker than they are. This can be a dangerous situation because now the bully feels as if he or she must prove something. So if you find yourself confronted or about to be confronted by a group, seek out the nearest adult and ask for their help. If you even suspect that something of this nature may be possible, don't walk into it. **TELL** an adult. That does not make you a coward.

That makes you a person with good common sense. You have much more to do with your time and life than to engage in arguments and street fights with people who are less than you are. If you even suspect that a group confrontation is a possibility while you are at school or some other public place, don't leave. Seek out an adult. Call the police. If you are already on the street step in to a store but seek HELP immediately. Don't be tricked into a confrontation. It's not worth it. You don't have to prove anything to anyone. In group confrontations it may look as if the world is against you. Just remember, the world is much bigger and much more than the group of small-minded, cowardly, bird-brains who are attempting to torment you. **TELL** and preserve yourself for the next step which is the real fight. If you are being bullied or if you know or suspect someone you know is being bullied in any way, get on the internet and get as much information as you can and then go to the school authorities and ask for help in forming an anti-bully peer organization. Once it's announced, you'll be surprised at how many other students will want to join and be a part of your group. In schools and community centers across the country victims of bullying and other concerned teens along with responsible adult sponsors are forming pro-active anti-bullying peer groups.

The bullied and those who care are rising up against the bully! And it's working! Again, the important thing is to SPEAK OUT.YOU ARE NOT ALONE! Organize and SPEAK OUT! It will help others and the bully will fade from your life. Remember, bullies are cowards with very low self-esteem. As a matter of fact, your anti-bullying organization may even help the bully to try and become a better person. How special would that be?

Love Always

DAY 11 JOURNAL

_____
_____
_____
_____
_____
_____
_____
_____
_____
_____
_____
_____
_____
_____
_____
_____
_____
_____
_____
_____
_____
_____

EMPOWERMENT DAY 12
By Kimberly Saul Whalen

PEER-PRESSURE

Dear Sweetheart,

My best advice for you today concerns peer-pressure. Overtime, I have learned many things about this subject, things I wish I had known when I was your age. However, even as I wish I could stop you from making some of the mistakes I made-as I now realize my mom tried to do with me—I also recognize that your life is your own and that you have to make your own mistakes. Even so, thank you so much for letting me share and perhaps some of what I've learned about peer-pressure will help you in your own very special journey. First and foremost, love yourself and be proud of who you are; a strong, confident and passionate young lady. One thing I know for sure is that it is more important to be true to yourself and your beliefs than it is to try to be someone or something you are not. At your age you have probably found that peer-pressure can often come from girls. But male or female it is important to define for

Yourself what a true friend is. It's not always the person you have the most fun with. In fact, I have learned that a true friend is there when there are more tears than laughter. A true friend is the one who accepts you no matter what. A true friend recognizes your faults and doesn't judge but, instead, cherishes your good qualities. A true friend always wants what is best for you and is happy for you when the best happens. A true friend will never pressure you to do something that makes you uncomfortable. A true friend brings out your best qualities. In life, you will have many, many acquaintances but we are lucky to have more than a few true friends. Actually only time will tell you who your true friends really are. One of my favorite quotes is by the author William Penn who wrote, "A true friend advises justly, assists readily, adventures boldly, takes all patiently, defends courageously and continues to be a friend unchangeably."

Unfortunately, a part of growing up and fitting in is how you look. It's too bad that society and the media put a great deal of emphasis on this. That's why it's so important for you to know, love and appreciate yourself. When peer-pressure arises, you will be able to stand firm and tall in what you believe. What I want you to know is, no matter what is seen on the outside, nothing can define who you are but you. When faced with any kind of peer-pressure from your girlfriends, boys or society, stay your authentic self. Stop and think. Anything that is in your best interest can wait. Then remember that the minute you entered this world you were special. Know that whether you're leading or a part of a group, you always want to be a positive and productive person. Be sure that you're being kind to others and treating them with the dignity and respect you expect for yourself. Always be compassionate to others but strong and confident about valuing your own inner beauty. Do these things and then you can listen to the whispers within when something doesn't seem quite right. You can listen to your gut when faced with difficult decisions.

Finally, always know that during every minute of every day for the rest of your life, there is someone who loves and adores you for the amazing person you are. Always remember that I am here for you as your mother and best friend without judgment and with unconditional love always and forever.

Love Always

DAY 12 JOURNAL

_____
_____
_____
_____
_____
_____
_____
_____
_____
_____
_____
_____
_____
_____
_____
_____
_____
_____
_____
_____
_____
_____
_____

EMPOWERMENT DAY 13

By Colleen S. Ward

SUICIDE

Dear Sweetheart,

My best advice for you today regarding suicide is this: First, before you try to end your life know that **I LOVE YOU, THAT YOU ARE SPECIAL, THAT YOU ARE UNIQUE. ONE-OF-A-KIND WONDERFUL!** You are my miracle created by God and given to me to love and cherish. Next, please know that Death IS FOREVER. You do not get to change your mind tomorrow. But know also that everything-every circumstance, good or bad, EVERYTHING changes—*except death*. So *as long as you are alive things will always get better*. **I PROMISE!** When you feel alone and over whelmed, take this letter out and read it again and give it one more day. Every time you do this you will get stronger and feel better. **I PROMISE!**

I can recall when I thought I could no longer take the reality of life so I called my grandmother to talk. As soon as I heard her voice I began to cry.

Grandma didn't ask what the problem was. *She told me that she loved me* just as I am telling you. She told me that God would never give me anything that I couldn't handle. And now I'm telling you. Brush away the dirt and debris and cobwebs and look for the signs that will guide you through life. They are all around you waiting for you. They are not for anyone else. You have a special purpose in this life that was designed for you and you alone and no one can fulfill that purpose but you. NO ONE.

Love Always

National Suicide Prevention Lifeline

1-800-273-8255

<u>Available 24 hours EVERYDAY!</u>

May God Continue To Bless Your Life!

DAY 13 JOURNAL

_____

_____

_____

_____

_____

_____

_____

_____

_____

_____

_____

_____

_____

_____

_____

_____

_____

_____

_____

_____

_____

_____

EMPOWERMENT DAY 14

By Sherri S. McArthur

DATING

Dear Sweetheart,

My best advice to you today regarding dating is to: ALWAYS maintain self-respect. When guys realize that you are a respectable young lady, they will know that their **"A-Game"** is a requirement and not an option. Boys actually WANT girls to have standards and guide lines for their behavior. Secondly, be clear why you are selecting a certain guy or a certain crowd. Are you just trying to fit in? Are you looking to fill some type of void in your life? Do you want someone to love you? To think you're special? Please know that these are things we all want. What you must do is increase your chances by BEING someone special—and it's not just about clothes and hair. Improve your grades. Develop a hobby. Play an instrument. Read a book. Take up a sport or start running or walking. Whatever you decide let it be something to improve you. The hardest one is this: Believe in yourself! When you feel good about yourself it will show and others will be drawn to you automatically. <u>You must love yourself before you can love</u>

someone else or expect them to love you.   Next, know that one of the most important element sofa relationship is friendship. When you feel comfortable enough to begin dating, choose a boyfriend who is true to the meaning that is a boy who is also your friend. Dating should be casual and fun and never thought of as a responsibility. You are not obligated to do anything that you don't want to do and keep in mind that bad decisions often follow you your entire life. The one thing you definitely have going for you is time. You don't have to rush into anything. Take your time. Select your friends and exercise your options with that thought in mind and never stray away from your personal values. This includes all of the people you associate with during your teen years. Always seek friendship first. Love and serious dating will have a much better chance. Finally, I want you to know how proud I am of you and that you are intelligent and beautiful inside and out. I believe you will continue to make good choices. I believe in you. Now, I want you to believe in yourself.

Love Always

DAY 14 JOURNAL

_____

_____

_____

_____

_____

_____

_____

_____

_____

_____

_____

_____

_____

_____

_____

_____

_____

_____

_____

_____

_____

_____

EMPOWERMENT DAY 15

By Corleen A. Piazza

SELF-ESTEEM

Dear Sweetheart,

My best advice for you today regarding self-esteem, my love, is this: As children we are taught to listen to the guidance of others. As we're growing up, each time and without even knowing it, we take what we're learning and we shift it, add to it, detract from it, shape and reshape the experience based on our own mental and emotional make up and then we come to various conclusions. Gradually, we take on more and more responsibility for ourselves, our opinions and decisions using the same process of shifting and shaping.

The answers we seek about what is right and true for our individual selves come now mostly from within. So even though there will always be self-help books, horoscopes and the advice of friends and family, begin to train yourself to listen to your own inner guide. Learn to trust in it and you will be on the true path to self-confidence and a healthy self-esteem. In today's world there is so much emphasis placed on youth and a perceived, perpetuated standard of beauty which actually leaves many of us on the side lines. We are bombarded with images of how we should look and dress every day.

However, if we listen to our inner voice which speaks from a basis of common sense and reality, we find that the true leaders of the world—in science, in industry, in medicine, in business, in education, in global affairs—in almost every field you can name, do not rely on that "perpetuated standard of beauty" to succeed. Develop your own standard of beauty, Sweetheart, based on the beauty in you. Put more emphasis on developing your character and personality; on learning and growing and expanding your horizons.

Learn from your mistakes and celebrate accomplishments—large and small. There are so many things to learn and do in this life. There are so many people to meet who are doing those interesting things in life. There are so many places to see, both in and out of America. You develop, maintain and boost your self-confidence by being your own best friend and by surrounding yourself with positive people, situations and environments. Incorporate these strategies into your life and watch your self-esteem soar! In the meantime, know today that you are already an amazing, dynamic individual destined to have an amazing dynamic future. So, get ready…set…Go! The world is yours!

Love Always

DAY 15 JOURNAL

EMPOWERMENT DAY 16

By Jacqueline A. Hawley

LOVE

Dear Sweetheart,

My best advice to you today concerns love. My cherished one, you will find that love is the favorite topic of many. You'll also find that when love is the topic, there will be as many different responses as there are people discussing it. It is the favorite subject of movies and books and songs. It seems to be the most used and misused word in any language AND the most important. Why? I think it is because love has so many variations in its meaning.

For example, there is love as the devotion and loyalty one feels for one's family. There is love as the warm and tender protective feeling one feels for a child. There is the great affection and friendship one feels for a friend. There is love as seen in the kindly benevolence of God and love as seen in the reverent devotion to God from us. There is the strong devotion for and to something such as "a love of books." The list goes on and on but it seems that the love that gets--requires--the most attention is the strong or passionate affection a person feels for someone they desire sexually. "Being in love" can be as confusing as it is wonderful because it has so much to do with the physical. A major portion of this letter is to stress how important it is to know and to SEPARATE THIS PHYSICAL FEELING FROM LOVE. At some point in your life they will combine, but not now. Not now. In the 1960's a phenomenal rock group called The Beatles took America by storm and sang in one of their more popular songs, "love is all you need." Everybody sang it because it was very romantic but it was also very misleading. At your age you also need information and clarification.

So here goes. You know how you have seen and felt your body changing over the last few years? Your breasts and the rest of your body are developing. You began your period. Hair has appeared or is beginning to appear on different sections of your body. When you look at your changing self you experience a number of new feelings including fear, pride and awe, don't you? Well, just as these physical changes have been happening on the outside where you could observe their progress just as many changes have been happening on the inside where you cannot openly observe and THEY ARE MORE IMPORTANT THAN THE ONES YOU CAN SEE! Yet, too often the outside evidence of these inside changes receives little or negative attention from the world around you. Some actions are reviewed as simple rebellion, among other things. I know sometimes it is scary but please know, the adults in your life are scared about those necessary changes they see in you too, afraid and reluctant to see their little girl move into the adult world. Be patient with us. We truly only want what is best for you. That is what this letter—this whole book—is about; YOU and helping YOU to understand what is happening to YOU. Your emotions, the way you feel, think and respond to life are all going through radical changes. Like the caterpillar and the butterfly you are changing daily but remember, the caterpillar crawls and the none day, as a butterfly, it flies. That's YOU. Moving toward maturity. A major part of that maturity will be your sexuality and how you think and respond to the physical urges your body expresses. Those feelings are okay. Fantasies are normal. Those feelings, those thoughts are all natural BUT please try hard not to confuse them with love. You will have pressure from all sides, including the twenty-four-hour bombardment of T.V., videos, songs, magazines and dozens of other media outlets. No matter how inviting and romantic they sound, **THAT'S ALL ABOUT MONEY**. This is about you and reality. Those physical urges are just that. Physical urges that we often attach to some person because that's a part of human nature and growing up too. PLEASE KNOW THAT. As hard as it may be sometimes, this is when it is most important to stop, think and listen to your head. You're smart. Listen. Love will always be in your life in one form or another because human beings need other human beings. Heading the list, though, should be a healthy love of self. If you have self-respect, you'll be able to respect others and others will respect you. If you know yourself, have balance between your inside self and your outside self, you won't be tricked into accepting physical attention from someone else as a substitute for love. If you surround yourself with the love of family, good friends, male and female, God and His world, you'll be ready later on when it is time for true physical love.

Love Always

DAY 16 JOURNAL

EMPOWERMENT DAY 17

By Leanne M. Estrella

PEER-PRESSURE

Dear Sweetheart,

My advice to you today concerns peer-pressure. One very important thing in your life to cultivate is learning how to choose friends. My mother always said, "dimeconquien andas y te diré quién eres." It means, <u>tell me who you are with and I will tell you who you are</u>. So, as you begin to enter the adult world, it is critical that you begin to know, first and foremost, just exactly who you are. Along with this self-discovery, finding true friendship is apart of your life time journey as you learn from trial and error. You will find that having fun with someone and enjoying their company does not make them your friend. True friends are there for you in the fun times as well as the not-so-fun times. True friends celebrate your achievements and stand with you when you have disappointments and failures. True friends listen. True friends always want what is best for you. True friends make you feel good about yourself and they always encourage you to develop the best part of you. If the person, male or female, does not fit this bill, he or she is not your friend but just an acquaintance. Whatever the relationship, it is important that you always be yourself. At the age you are now, you are most likely involved in an organization or group at school. This is an important way for you to discover what activities you enjoy and an important part of figuring out who you are. However, sometimes when we are apart of a group, we feel the urge to be like everyone else so that we will be liked. This is human nature. Everyone wants to be accepted and liked. But I encourage you today to not just settle for "being like everyone else." Be yourself! "Being like everyone else" will cause you to miss out on so many wonderful experiences and opportunities that the unique and only you would have found open to her. We are all different in many ways and that's what makes us the unique individuals that we are. Make an effort to find out what your uniqueness is and begin to develop those traits in a positive way. Make your uniqueness work for you. In other words, be yourself and life will be more enjoyable and every experience will be beneficial. Growing up in a Latin house hold provided the foundation for the values and opinions I now have as an adult. For example, my culture is full of tradition and proper etiquette for addressing others. Respect was one of the big ones. Ever since I can remember, I was always taught to address adults and strangers in a certain way. This and many other parts of the value system that has sustained me were often the total opposite of what the media and my peers thought were acceptable. I had to learn as I hope you will learn that what "everybody else did" was not me. Developing this mind set made me a stronger, happier person and I know if you embrace your own uniqueness it will do the same for you. No, it will not be easy—but think about it. Do you really want to just be a follower? Or do you dare to stand up for what you believe, feel and know is right? Do you really want to just follow the crowd and act and dress a certain way just because "everyone is doing it?" I don't think so. I think you want to form your own very special and unique identity by making choices that are right for you. Yes, you may be teased or mocked but at the end of the day you will appreciate not simply being a follower. As Malcolm X said, "If you don't stand for something, you will fall for anything." This definitely applies to peer-pressure. Finally, never, ever take part in putting others down. In addition to just being wrong, teasing and bullying others is the strongest evidence of the lowest self-esteem. Being an individual with your own thoughts and views is what makes you YOU! You are an original. Don't be afraid to follow your destiny and show the world!

Love Always

DAY 17 JOURNAL

EMPOWERMENT DAY 18

By Gwendolyn B. Walker

DATING

Dear Sweetheart,

Welcome to another beautiful, God given day! My best advice for you today concerning dating is, please recognize your own value and your own personal beauty inside and out before becoming involved in this area. Enjoy self-discovery and the fun and fellowship of friends and family before serious dating. My personal recommendation would be that you wait for one-on-one dating until you are in your late teens. However, whenever you start to date, the following advice still stands. Guard your heart and don't give it away to just any young man who likes you and wants to spend time with you. Trust me, there will be so many others. Keep your eyes wide open and your mind alert. Don't look at the outward appearance only but see what is inside as well. It will be visible through his words and actions toward you and others. Think about the character and values these behaviors communicate about this young man. Think about how this compares with the person you are and the person you aspire to be. Is he a giver or a taker?

Is he thoughtful or inconsiderate? Is he kind hearted or mean spirited? Is he respectful of your parents 'rules for spending time with you? Do you feel respected and valued after spending time with him? Only after honestly answering these questions should you decide to open or close your schedule (time) and your heart (affection) to a young man. You notice I used the word "decide." It is YOUR life and YOUR decision. If you decide he is worthy, don't rush ahead to become the pursuer. Remain the person being pursued. Let him ask you for your phone number. Let him call you. Let him ask your parents' permission to take you out. Let him plan and pay for the date. Let him come to your door to pick you up, not honk for you to come out. *What you can do is be respectful of yourself and him in the way you behave and dress while dating*. Allow the young man to engage with your parents without feeling that you need to protect him or explain them. Your parents know and love you and want the best for you. Be wise and consider their counsel. It's their job to give it. Keep in mind that YOU are the prize to be pursued. Allow only worthy young men to pursue you and attempt capturing your heart. Remember, things that come too easily are often valued least. This is especially true with regards to dating. I pray you feel the love of this advice.

Love Always

DAY 18 JOURNAL

EMPOWERMENT DAY 19

By Latoria T. Polite

SEX vs. ABSTINENCE

Dear Sweetheart,

My best advice to you today concerns sex versus abstinence. As girls and young women we have been led to believe many things about sex that are untrue or only partly true. Because of this and because I love you so much, today I would like to set the record straight. In our pre-teens, sex often begins as just a matter of curiosity. As we move into and through our teen years that curiosity is consistently enhanced and encouraged by overwhelming media exposure, our imaginations and the most powerful stimuli of all, our changing body and physical needs. Sometimes it's frightening, sometimes it is exciting and sometimes it's both. Whatever the case may be, ***know this– it's natural***. It may also help to know you are going through what millions of women all over the world have gone through since the beginning of time. The big secret is what should you do about it? First, I suggest separating the truth about sex from the perception that society gives. You see, in one way or another, we are constantly being told that sex will lead to a successful relationship; that it will boost our popularity; that it will make us feel more like a woman. The truth is **SEX BY ITSELF IS PURELY PHYSICAL**. Science says that next to hunger, sex is the most critical animal urge. Knowing that the urge to have sex is just as natural as having the urge to eat, you have to decide what role sex is going to play in your life and stand firm on your decision. Psychologically speaking, what you think, you feel, and what you feel, you do. This cycle is supported by an underlining belief system or set of values that you have to set for yourself. No matter how difficult, what you DO is controlled by YOU and shouldn't be left for society or anyone else to decide. Society says, "Use protection," or "wrap it up." What society fails to tell you is there is no protection against the heart break you'll feel when you and that person break up.

The media says do what makes you feel good while movies portray the pinnacle of every relationship as being the moment you have sex. They don't point out that the movies you're watching have cameras and directors telling the actors what to do next and what emotions to portray. The actors are PAID to act a certain way. In real life there is no script, no one to control your sexual partner; no one to tell either of you what

86

to do next. The media may show you the morning after sex having a glamorous breakfast in bed. **You have to know this is fantasy.** What they'll fail to tell you about is the let down; empty feeling you will have after the act and the degradation and shame *you will feel* because you'll wish you had waited. You'll know, AFTER WARDS, it was just a physical act not attached to anything valuable or the future you want for yourself.

The media won't show you the years you'll spend and the time you'll waste trying to find yourself after realizing you have given a very sacred part of who you are and what you possess to boy after boy after boy in meaningless physical sex. Once you have had sex, ___*it's not impossible to stop*___ but the physical and psychological urges will increase and the harder it will be to practice abstinence. Yes, sex is natural and important. Yes, sex is a big deal and can be a beautiful, wonderful experience. BUT-sex is also extremely intimate. Don't dilute it. Don't waste it. You are who you say you are. So if you want to be respected, valued, and unconditionally loved, BE STINGY WITH YOURSELF. Think and reason. Take this time to learn who you are. Take this time to grow into who you will eventually become. Take this time to determine the kind of guy who will deserve you and who you will choose because you know he will cherish the beautiful jewel that you are. I personally believe that remaining abstinent until marriage is best. I promise you will thank me later!

Love Always

DAY 19 JOURNAL

EMPOWERMENT DAY 20

By Carmen Carter Cody

RELATIONSHIPS

Dear Sweetheart,

My best advice for you today regarding relationships comes from our story. It was just like yesterday that I held you in my arms. Today, I look with awe at the beautiful and intelligent young lady that you have become. However, even as you grow and mature, I will always want to share all that I have with you. Over the years, I have watched our relationship change from my being a nurturer and protector at your birth, to an observer as you discovered how to walk, to a health teacher as you entered puberty, to an advisor and counselor as high school came into sight. That's what I want to share with you today. Relationships change and the most critical, the most valuable element in that change is **TRUST**. As a person travels through their teenage years, certain relationships may become a challenge. I want you to know that that's natural. It's a part of growing up. As an infant, toddler, and preteen your full trust was in me.

You did not doubt for a moment that I was going to feed you, cloth you and otherwise provide for you in all ways. As you begin to move toward adulthood, you also begin to have your own thoughts about how things should be done; you naturally begin to develop your own ideas and opinions about life; you begin the long, exciting, slightly scary but wonderful, journey toward becoming uniquely YOU! The key word here, of course, is BEGIN.

You are BEGINNING. In these teenage years, the first step toward really becoming an adult is knowing this. It is realizing that you are still a child; that you still need to trust final judgments and decisions to those who have brought you safely this far. Becoming an adult is to first realize that your parents love you and want only what is right and good for you. Yes, I will make mistakes but at this time of your life, I wish, I hope, I TRUST that you will see that it is better to be my mistake than yours.

My dear, enjoy your childhood but know that at this point so much of our relationship, how I treat you, depends upon you and your growing maturity. It is my job to watch, continue to protect and guide you through that development and to the door step of your adult life. Think of this: You want me to TRUST you to go out with your friends, hangout at the mall, to eventually drive MY car. As a parent, I'm watching your day-to-day actions. Are you doing your chores well and without being reminded or hounded? Are you keeping up your grades realizing the important part this will play in your future life? Are you talking back or showing other signs of disrespect? Are you being self-centered and defiant like the little kid you no longer want to be? Can I TRUST you to make the most responsible decision possible when faced with uncertain circumstances and peer-pressure? All of these things and more MUST be in place before I can release you to soar to the heights that I know you are capable of.

Sweetheart, there are so many others involved in this process of give and take and TRUST but over the next few years some of the most important are your teachers. Know this. Your relationship with your teachers is similar to the relationship with your parents. The budding adult in you will realize that your teachers are human too and will make mistakes but that they are on your side. Their job is to help prepare you to become the most effective adult you're capable of becoming.

Once you embrace this, you will always strive to do your best, to respect the rules of your school and class room; you will keep communication lines open between you and your teachers, doing what you are asked to do as well as those things you know you are supposed to do and asking, in a mature responsible way, when you have questions or are not sure. A book can be written on the importance of communicating alone, but you're a smart girl. You get the idea. As I close my letter to you, I TRUST that you will see that all I do I do with you in mind. Since you were born that has been and continues to be the essence of our relationship.

Making and learning from mistakes is an important part of growing up and of life but I do want you to avoid making as many mistakes as possible that I and others have made. Try to tread on higher ground. Stand on my shoulders and reach your destiny beyond the stars. I love you, my beloved daughter.

Love Always

DAY 20 JOURNAL

_____

_____

_____

_____

_____

_____

_____

_____

_____

_____

_____

_____

_____

_____

_____

_____

_____

_____

_____

_____

_____

_____

_____

_____

EMPOWERMENT DAY 21

By Jessie Johnson

ABUSE

Dear Sweetheart,

The subject of my best advice to you today is drug and alcohol abuse. I am advising you to do one of the simplest, hardest things you will do in your life and that is, be smart enough to JUST SAY NO! This is another one of those life situations where there is no compromise. It is too important. JUST SAY NO! You are almost grown up and beginning to make choices and decisions for yourself. This letter, my love, is to convince you--assure you--that, this time, there really is a big ugly monster out there waiting to destroy your life. There really is a monster connected to the use of drugs and the abuse of alcohol that you must be aware of, that you must be afraid of, that you must run hard and fast from and its name is ADDICTION. This monster is sneaky. One day it is innocent fun and the next day your life is not your own. This monster is vicious. Its job is to destroy--to destroy your ability to think rationally, to destroy your health, your chance for happiness and your future. This monster's job is to alienate you from family, true friends and healthy relationships. This monster is a killer of life, hopes and dreams. I know because I've been there for too much of my life and because I love you and pray you will be smarter than I was, I take this time to tell you a little of my story. I grew up in a two-parent household where love was evident and I knew it. As far back as I can remember I always wanted to become a nurse. I loved their sparkling white uniforms and the service they provided. I dreamed many days of helping any and everyone. That was what motivated me to keep my grades high. From kindergarten through 12th grade there was no substance abuse in my life. During my second year of college, I dropped my guard, became curious and began experimenting with drugs and alcohol. CURIOSITY ABOUT SOME THINGS CAN BE DANGEROUS! There are some things that are not worth your time, energy, efforts, money or life. JUST SAY NO! I didn't and one day I met a guy who introduced me to powder cocaine. He told me he loved me and would never leave me. Ten years later, he was gone and I had progressed to crack cocaine. I was addicted for the next

18 years in which time I became everything I hated--a liar, a thief, a manipulator and a cheater. All I cared about was one more "hit" or drink. I spent my days and nights walking the streets, jumping in and out of men's cars, not caring

96

about what would happen to me and allowing myself to be treated as less than a person. All relationships were superficial. I was mentally and physically degraded and abused and I didn't care because ADDICTION was my God and I did what it demanded that I do. After my last boyfriend tried to strangle me to death, I found the strength, the courage to give it all up. I walked away with the only book I had and it was a Bible. I had my father's picture. I held on to it for encouragement and, by the way, my father died during my ADDICTION and he never got a chance to see his little girl in her right mind again. Every time I think of that, I cry. However, in rehabilitation I relearned that I was not a bad person. I was a sick person and the name of this very contagious disease is ADDICTION. I have restructured my life and today have a good job and a strong support network. Staying free, of course, is a daily fight but I know now that I have always had a choice--to use or not to use--and that is your choice, Sweetheart. Vow to live your life. Don't waste years rebuilding it. Please, be smart enough, strong enough, to choose wisely and JUST SAY NO!

Love Always

DAY 21 JOURNAL

EMPOWERMENT DAY 22

By Dedria D. Price

DATING

Dear Sweetheart,

Please begin this day knowing you are loved and cherished. My best advice for the day concerns dating and it is this: If you are under 17, GROUP DATE ONLY! Dating at any age can and should be fun but before 17 it should be about going places and doing fun things with other young people you know, respect and enjoy being with. These should be young people whose value system mirrors your own, who respect themselves and others. It's a time for finding out who you really are and BEGINNING to make decisions about yourself, your standards and beliefs that may impact the rest of your life. *There is no magic age but, hopefully, by age 17 you will have matured enough to single date even though I still recommend that you group date as much as possible*. Why? Because you have your whole life ahead of you--a life that you should be preparing for with schooling, adventures and simply living. Why force yourself to begin making life choices that you are not equipped to make and that you don't HAVE to make at this time? You will find many, many adults who wish they had taken or could have taken the opportunity to finish growing up. On the other hand, you will find very few adults, if any, who are happy that they rushed through childhood to adulthood.

Before you move on to one-on-one dating, be certain that you have a healthy respect for who and what you are, how you expect to be treated and an iron-clad value system that cannot be shaken.

Lastly, but certainly not least, go into all relationships with God as your anchor. **Prayer is a powerful tool. Please learn to use it.**

Love Always!

DAY 22 JOURNAL

EMPOWERMENT DAY 23

By Natassia Schumpert

PEER-PRESSURE

Dear Sweetheart,

My advice to you today concerns peer-pressure. I'm so happy to be able to do that by sharing parts of my own story with you. Growing up in my high school I thought being popular was important because I wanted people to like me and I wanted to have fun and be considered "cool." What I finally discovered was that being popular can be both positive and negative. Being popular because you are well known for standing up for the right thing is positive. Being popular because you always go along with the group even if the members are wrong is negative.

In my search for popularity, I dealt with plenty of peer-pressure. There were times when I allowed myself to be pressured into smoking weed and afterwards felt guilty every time because originally I had not wanted to do it. There were times I was made fun of because I had not had sex and wanted to save that part of myself for adulthood and marriage. I knew many girls who were contracting STD'S, becoming pregnant, having abortions and so forth and I did not want any part of it. I was pressured from all sides. I was told to just have sex instead of waiting for the right guy because it wasn't that serious to them. It was just sex. I was also told to just go have sex with someone I could meet at the club and get it over with. Well, I thank God every day that I did not fall into any of those traps. I became aware that these people were not my true friends and that I should have walked away from them and cut them out of my life sooner than I did. I realized that they were attempting to poison my mind with lies and myths that were all dangerous pitfalls. Maybe they didn't know it themselves but they were actually hungry to set me up for failure.

The most important thing though was I began to realize it for myself. I think I began to grow up. So even though I was well known, I chose to avoid negative popularity. I didn't like the way it felt. I chose not to be "cool" because I would not bow to peer-pressure but chose instead to follow my own heart and try always to do the right thing. The key words here are, "I chose." That was the way I was raised and I always felt good about myself when I did what I knew to be right. I hope this is what you will choose for

103

yourself in the days ahead. You will never regret it. As I grew older, I found that those negative popular people grew to be less and less important, especially after we graduated from high school and we all had to face the real world. In a few years as you move into the adult world the things you do in high school will fade away and become a blur but they will have established the foundation for the kind of person you will eventually grow into. Begin to choose well now. I have heard plenty of stories about those kids from my teenage years who were mean but popular while in school and who, now have sad, sad stories.

Many are among strippers, drunks, abusers, cheaters, liars, fighters, in and out of jail or on drugs. Some however have managed to turn their lives around by taking a good look at themselves and finally realizing that their problem was their own lack of self-esteem and that you don't have to bully and put other people down to be liked and respected. You get true respect when you respect the rights of others. Anything else is time wasted. The prom queen won't wear her crown past prom night. Prom king does not wear his crown past prom night. Friends go their separate ways and those who are your real friends will still be there. Often, peer-pressure and abusive relationships come disguised as friendship but please hear me, today.

It's only peer-pressure in its most negative form. If the friend takes advantage of you or always makes you feel down, that's not friendship, that's peer-pressure. If someone tries to talk you into doing things that you do not want to do even after you tell them how you feel, that's not friendship. That's peer-pressure. If someone disrespects your beliefs or morals or values, that's not friendship.

It's peer-pressure. If someone tells you to cheat or drink or have sex for whatever reason, recognize that it is a trap and your life is much more valuable than a one-night stand, a sip of liquor, a hit of weed or some other drug. Don't be tempted into experimenting with your life. Love yourself too much for that. Know who you are and protect who you are. Put your foot down, hold your head up young lady and know that you are loved, you are of value, you have worth and you are not for sale because you are not an item. You are a very special individual who knows the value of friends but refuses to be a pawn for anyone. And you know what, Sweetheart? It's really so simple. All you have to do is do what you know to be right and always, always treat everyone the way you want to be treated. It's the golden rule because it is the most important rule to follow all through your life. I ask God to protect you from all negative pressures of this world and I pray you will always surround yourself with positive people. It's the key to success and happiness. Wear it close to your heart and use it to unlock doors to a happy, healthy, joy-filled life.

Love Always

DAY 23 JOURNAL

EMPOWERMENT DAY 24

By Clovice Ramsey

SELF-ESTEEM

Dear Sweetheart,

My best advice for you today concerns self-esteem. Our perceptions of ourselves are mostly shaped by others and too often they stop with the physical. But let's look at that for a moment. Have you ever considered that the rarest gems are the most valuable? That the most coveted collections in the world contain one of a kind objects? Well, that's you, one of a kind. A rare, valuable, coveted masterpiece. Since the beginning of time until the end of time there will never, ever be anyone who looks, thinks, walks, talks, laughs, cries, feels, exactly like you! No one can beat you at being you and how you perceive yourself inside your heart and head will manifest itself in how you present yourself and respond to the world. Can you begin to appreciate that? I understand that the singer, Barbara Streisand was once advised to have cosmetic surgery on her nose which did not fit someone's idea of beauty. She was a fabulous singer; she had youth, fame and fortune. She could have done it but she refused. Why? I imagine because that nose was uniquely hers and therefore she valued it. She had very high self-esteem which was not based upon anyone else's opinion of her looks. She had her God given talent; she was educated, sophisticated, kind, generous and beautiful in her own right. I wish I had known about Barbara Streisand when I was a teen. I used to be so self-conscious. I was called everything from Brick-house to Stallion to Miss. Clydesdale. I would wear long sweaters in 90-degree weather in an attempt to hide my body. I let other people define me and I was miserable. As I matured I began to realize that God does not make mistakes and that I am, as the scriptures states, *"fearfully and wonderfully made."* I began to appreciate my body as God's special handiwork and not as some mythical representation of what "everybody" should look like. I want you to know that wanting to be and look like everyone else is still apart of being a teenager in America today. But know also that this should and will pass and that this letter, along with my love, is meant as a tool to help you to and through that transition. In the meantime, explore and then begin to expand the "uniqueness" in yourself by cultivating a clean, healthy body, a clean, healthy mind and a clean, healthy spirit.

At the same time, take a look at the world around you and beyond and begin to decide how you are going to use that very special "uniqueness" of yours to add to, impact, influence, and maybe even, change the world. Now take that, lift your head up high and go out and have a wonderful day!

Love Always

DAY 24 JOURNAL

EMPOWERMENT DAY 25

By Monica Noreen Lockrem

FEAR

Dear Sweetheart,

My best advice for you today concerns fear. You are about to enter a very exciting and wonderful phase of your life. Ahead lies many ups and downs; many obstacles, challenges and changes. Too often these will be accompanied by fear. So the first thing I want to say to you is, fear is natural. It's an emotion to be experienced like happiness and sadness. And Sweetheart, if you are ever with someone who says they are not afraid of anything, be very cautious of them. There are many positive aspects to fear.

Fear often acts as a safeguard letting you know you are in danger. Sometimes fear acts as a signal that you need to prepare more for what you are about to undertake. On the other hand, fear can also be a boogeyman who saps your confidence and prevents you from being the strong, creative individual I know you are destined to be. That's why I feel the subject is so important. Do you remember the first time you rode a bike without training wheels? Do you remember the first day of kindergarten? Can you remember watching a scary movie and being afraid of the dark? All of those were fearful times, weren't they? Now, thinking back, I'll bet those moments don't seem like such a big deal after all. A great man in history named Winston Churchill once told a nation, "You have nothing to fear but fear itself."

This is the first thing you should know about fear. Although being afraid is natural and many times helpful, it's what you DO when fear strikes you that's the most important thing to think about. You see fear can be a bully too. So even when faced with fear, the primary thing to remember is YOU are the one in charge. Don't let fear take that away from you. You can be afraid and decide to be a coward or you can do what you know is right and be a hero no matter how hard it is. You can be afraid and turn back or take the warning and move ahead with courage and caution as your guides. You can be afraid and give up or arm yourself with the necessary information and tools, throw your shoulders back and push ahead. You can be afraid and hang your head in shame or you can remind yourself that you are a very special, unique, one of a kind individual who has much to offer and take your rightful place up front. Finally, you will make mistakes. Everyone does. Sometimes you will have to stop and start again. The big point here to remember is NEVER, EVER let fear be your only guide.

Love Always

DAY 25 JOURNAL

_____

_____

_____

_____

_____

_____

_____

_____

_____

_____

_____

_____

_____

_____

_____

_____

_____

_____

_____

_____

_____

_____

_____

_____

EMPOWERMENT DAY 26

By LaToyia D. Jones

SUICIDE

Dear Sweetheart,

My best advice to you today regarding suicide is this: YES! sometimes it seems as if certain problems or difficulties in our lives are much more than we can bear BUT—please listen to me closely—LIVING YOUR LIFE IS OF FAR GREATER VALUE THAN DEATH! Have you ever considered that your life was created to make an impact on this world? That there is someone who is waiting for YOU to LIVE? Turn around. Now focus really hard with everything that is in you. Don't you see them? Don't you see all the girls and women who are waiting for you to accomplish all the things you were created to accomplish? They are eager to witness your story and your courage as you handle the trials, storms and road blocks in your life so that they can draw from your example and in turn make their own special contribution when the time comes. I can share this with you because I remember hitting a serious road block when I was a teenager and wishing that my life would end.

As I looked to my left and to my right all I could see were people who seemed to be against me and situations that seemed bigger and taller than I was. I felt as if LIFE was not worth living and that it would never get any better. I can remember lying in bed with a plastic bag and a razor trying to figure out which was the quickest and least painful way to exit this earth. I was fifteen years old. Guess what happened next? In my mind, I had a vision and felt myself being tapped from behind. In the vision, I turned and there was a young lady waiting patiently to see what I was going to do next.

As we stared at each other my eyes filled with tears because I realized that I could not let her down, that I had to give it at least one more day, that LIFE was worth living at least for that day. That day eventually turned into weeks, weeks into months, months into years and years into now. And now I can stand here today knowing that it was worth it because wherever else this life journey has taken me, It has given me YOU and you are worth everything. So, as I softly tap you on the shoulder, I say to you, YOUR LIFE IS WORTH LIVING! Others are waiting. There is no trial that you cannot handle and no situation that you do not have the strength to face if you just believe in yourself. YOU ARE STRONGER THAN YOU THINK. How do I know this? Because you are God's creation and the last time I checked, He wasn't making anything less than amazing. So, I challenge you to discover the courage, the strength, the tenacity and the fight to push through LIFE with all that you have and to reach the other side of this obstacle ALIVE and with purpose.

Love Always

National Suicide Prevention Lifeline

1-800-273-8255

<u>Available 24 hours EVERYDAY!</u>

May God Continue To Bless Your Life!

DAY 26 JOURNAL

_____

_____

_____

_____

_____

_____

_____

_____

_____

_____

_____

_____

_____

_____

_____

_____

_____

_____

_____

_____

_____

_____

EMPOWERMENT DAY 27

By Carla J. Tibbs

RELATIONSHIPS

Dear Sweetheart,

My best advice for you today regarding relationships is this: Life is a process and relationships are a part of that process so take your time with both and enjoy the journey. You know, when we are young our vision is so "future focused." We tend to rush through the "right now," but there is a saying in carpentry and in sewing that you should consider making one of your life mottos and that is **"measure twice and cut once."** That is, take the time to evaluate every situation before you take that part of your journey.

I cannot stress enough how important measuring is, how absolutely necessary it is in order to get the best possible out of this life. And, YES, it is also time consuming--BUT--if you are in too much of a hurry, you may end up "cutting" too soon or just cutting wrong, meaning, taking action that cannot be taken back. When you are measuring, you can adjust, rethink, strategize, compare, compromise, plan, restructure or completely abandon a thought, a whim or a potential action. Once you have made that "cut" or taken that irrevocable action, you cannot take it back. You are committed to your decision whether the decision later proves right or wrong, weak or strong. Actually, this applies to relationships and all of life. Now, our very first relationship is with our parents. As we grow from child to teen to adult, the relationship gradually changes. As we mature our participation in the process becomes more and more vital. So, since you, my daughter, are in the process of joining the adult world, realize that communication is the key to keeping this critical relationship intact and strong. I love you. Unequivocally. I do understand. However, everyone is not a strong communicator. Your maturity will allow you to become a part of the "give and take" in our relationship. Try "measuring" where we adults are coming from. We are not trying to ruin your life. We are looking back. It is said that hind sight is 20/20.

You might not be able to see certain things now but we know if you make that wrong step, move or "cut" too soon, years later the mistake and the better choice will become crystal clear in hind sight. No, I cannot live your life for you.

Yes, you will have to experience many heartaches that I will not be able to buffer but give me a break. Why make unnecessary mistakes and engage in unnecessary pain? Be smart. Please take the time to listen and I promise I will do everything in my power to hear you and your heart. The same principal applies to you and your friends who have siblings.

For example, when you are faced with a ball coming straight at you your natural reaction is to dodge it, right? However, if you are playing a sport and dodge or just react you will not meet whatever your objective is. You must know when to catch, when to throw, bat, volley, shoot, dodge or run. It depends on your desired result which action you respond with. Siblings are friends who last a life time but like any relationship, it takes work. Maturity means we can begin to see things from our sibling's vantage point an instead of just reacting we begin to respond to them with a desired result in mind. I use the word "maturity" often in this letter because it is a good yardstick for measuring your progress.

As we mature we should also be aware of or look out for "warnings" or "signs" in all of our relationships. If you look at the sky and see dark clouds and lightning and hear thunder you know you need to take cover because there is a good possibility of rain. There are always signs and warnings to help guide us through relationships. We just need to be open to them and heed them. Why wait for the rain to soak us before we seek shelter? In other words, If you hear the warnings of a parent, a teacher, a friend or those coming from your own head and heart because of the actions of another, listen and get out of the rain! Finally, some say "what you don't know won't hurt you." Sorry, Sweetheart. What you don't know can alter your life forever. When the storms of life are clamoring all around you, a voice from a parent or loved one can save your day, your future, your life. Respect the voices of those close to you who care for you. Respect those who have gone before you and are where you want to be. Respect the voice of one who is not where you want to be when that person is telling you how to avoid their mistakes. Listen, prepare, measure the circumstances in any relationship. You're young so take your time and move slowly. Enjoy, enjoy, enjoy your life! But always, always, always consider consequences before taking any action with or for anyone and remember, the beauty of a young woman is unmatched when it is coming from her own self-respect. Let this thought guide you in all relationships.

Love Always

DAY 27 JOURNAL

EMPOWERMENT DAY 28

By Shannon Michelle Conley

BULLYING

Dear Sweetheart,

My best advice to you today concerns bullying. I pass on to you the advice that was given to me by my favorite grandfather, words that I have lived by since he said them to me when I was in grade school. He said, "Never back down from a bully!" There was more said to me but that is the one liner that I want you to remember. Why you should never back down from a bully can be narrowed down to one significant difference between you and the bully and that is *"Courage versus Cowardliness."*

The reasons why a bully is a bully are not necessarily your concern but there's a good chance if you knew some of them you would feel sorry for him or her. Whatever it was destroyed their self-esteem. Bullying others is how they hope to hide it. The bottom line is bullies do not like themselves and they spend a lot of time trying to make others feel as worthless and insecure as they feel. However, when the bullied stands up to the bully it is something that is not expected.

The bully normally backs down because standing your ground takes courage which is something every bully lacks. Here's a story: When I was about nine years old, my mother, my younger sister and I were going back to our car from grocery shopping. My little sister started to get scared and upset when she saw her bully in the parking lot. My mother sensed that she needed to step in but I said to my Mom, "Grandpa told me to never back down from a bully.

So let me take care of it." I was scared of course and this bully was twice my size but I wanted to be the hero in my little sister's eyes so I got right between that big old bully and my sister and pointing my finger at her I said, "My Grandpa taught me to never back down from a bully and you are a bully! You leave my sister alone!" And that was that! The bully was totally perplexed and had no idea how to respond because someone stood up to her. From that day on, she gave my sister no more problems. Yes, I faced bullies in middle school and many times since, but I never backed down. I held my head high and kept my focus on important things like my studies. The bullies never went to college. They invariably got into trouble and still remain quite miserable people. Always remember, life has a funny way of rewarding those who treat others with kindness and those who continue to persevere without hurting others on the journey. As long as you speak up for what you stand for and remain steadfast in your values and morals, no bully can beat you because no bully can take that away from you. Also, when you tell a bully he or she is wrong and you are not going to stand for it, most of the time it scares them away.

So say it loud and say it proud, **"I don't back down from bullies!"** I pray this letter encourages you today to keep your head up and stay proud of who and what you are and always know that I love you and that I am proud of you just as you are!

Love Always

DAY 28 JOURNAL

EMPOWERMENT DAY 29

By Deana E. Montgomery

SEX vs. ABSTINENCE

Dear Sweetheart,

My best advice for you today deals with sex versus abstinence as well as some words of encouragement in case you or any of your friends are, for whatever reason, dealing with a premature sexual experience. Contemporary culture promotes having sex as the "in" thing to do but losing your virginity is a life altering experience. Don't let friends, a boy, the media or your body fool you. The very safest, wisest thing to do is to avoid the sexual experience until you are fully grown up and leading an informed, independent, married life. Premature sex can come about in so many different ways. It can happen with someone you care so deeply about that you make the decision to let your heart (the physical) overrule your head. It can happen in a moment of bad judgment with someone you barely know. More tragically, it can happen as a result of rape or incest. Whichever the case, after the act the girl is always left with a combination of feelings including shame, guilt, regret, depression and, sometimes, desperation. Please know this, although once you lose your virginity it is gone forever, you can still recover your self-respect, happiness and hope for the future. You never stop with a bad experience. Use it to guide and sustain you in the future. Although it may be hard at times, **abstinence** is the best practice. I strongly believe that the ideal time to become sexually active is inside the love, security, and commitment of **marriage**. The choice is yours; please choose wisely.

Talk to an adult that you trust; focus on your education, get involved in school activities, as well as, church and local youth organizations. Avoid sexually stimulating situations. The main thing to do is to plan positive activities and to keep busy. Don't concentrate on what is behind you but, rather, what is ahead of you. Make a conscious choice to practice abstinence for the next few years of your life. Sexual abstinence means not having any type of intercourse or sex play. REMEMBER, it is your choice and your choice alone. If, on the other hand, you have been forced into having sex, please know that you are not at fault. **Tell someone immediately**, your parents or guardians, a school counselor, spiritual leader, or some other adult that you trust. Always remember, **your life is not over**

I am a life coach to women who have been sexually abused. Countless times, through prayer and counseling I have seen women transform their lives by learning how to process the injuries that they have suffered.

Many have regained their dignity, their strength and their voices and are living healthy, productive lives. God forbid but if this ever becomes your experience, remember you still have the ability to soar, to triumph. <u>Forge ahead, discover your destiny, and take hold of all of the great things that lie ahead of you.</u>

Love Always

DAY 29 JOURNAL

EMPOWERMENT DAY 30

By Vanessa Rice

MONEY

Dear Sweetheart,

My best advice for you today concerns money. Honey, the subject is as hard to talk about as it is important to understand. It's pretty obvious why it's important to talk about, isn't it? We are surrounded, day and night, with things to buy, things that cost money. Some of them, like shelter, food and clothing, we need but most of them, even under those categories, are designed and promoted to simply make money for someone else. That's something you should think about every time you consider buying something that you've seen advertised. And that leads to what makes the importance of money so hard to talk about. Some media person is always trying to convince you to spend money on something, right? Well, it's at this point in your life that you need to begin thinking about what you want to spend money on and not what someone tells you you should spend money on because it will make you pretty or popular or acceptable.

And one of the most stupid reasons for spending money that a lot of adults fall into is keeping up with what somebody else has or is doing. Too often the flash and dash of television and movies, the commercials that say buy, buy, buy mislead people into thinking that money must be the answer to all problems. This is wrong and untrue. As a matter of fact, many crimes are committed because people begin to believe that money is the key to happiness or the answer to whatever problems they have.

All day, every day people are ruining their lives to get instant money for things they're not willing to work and save for and, most often, don't even need. The job of advertising is to make you want something even if you don't need it and can't afford it. But honey, you're smart enough to know that the sports figures and entertainers with lavish wealth that you see and hear about all the time are in the minority. Most people on earth are **_not_** rich but most of them are leading happy, productive lives. They're able to do this because, even though they have sense enough to know that in this day and age it takes money to live, they also know that money in itself will not guarantee love or happiness or strength of character or good health or any of the other assets that will lead to a balanced, fulfilled and joyous life.

From childhood, the musical genius, Michael Jackson, could buy anything he wanted. He had the money but it did not in sure his happiness. He died too young and under terrible conditions. Money did not save him or make his life happy. Think about it. On the other hand, it's never too early to look for ways to earn your own money. Young people as well as adults who earn their own money are usually more conscious and careful about how they spend it. Neither is it too early to set goals, no matter how small, for spending or getting what you want. This will require saving and budgeting and will make you greatly appreciate whatever you decide to buy.

Believe me, the things we strive and work for, we appreciate most. Now, one of the first signs of your growing maturity over the next few years will be your understanding of the need to plan fora future of financial self-sufficiency. Being financially strong and independent should certainly be one of your life goals but always remember that you must keep money in prospective. Try making a list of all the things that you cannot buy that could make a person happy. Make a scrap book of pictures or a wall collage. Write a poem or a song. Make your own advertisement about the companion piece to financial wealth.

Study it. Add to it. Treasure it. There are many times in life when money might not be there to sustain you. Those things you have recorded will. Listen! *By all means plan to make money* in life but remember, **_never, ever let money make you._**

Love Always

DAY 30 JOURNAL

EMPOWERMENT DAY 31

By Mavis Colleen Hill

ENTREPRENEURSHIP

Dear Sweetheart,

My best advice for you today concerns entrepreneurship. The dictionary definition of an entrepreneur is *"a person who organizes and manages a business or industrial empire."* Too often when we think of entrepreneurship the one that comes to mind is the one closest to the industrial empire. The reason I have chosen to write to you about entrepreneurship today is because I feel it is not talked about to young people enough and because of the very critical place entrepreneurship holds in history and in all levels of societies everywhere. For example, do you have a friend who does hair or nails for family and friends to make extra money? That's a form of entrepreneurship. Do you know someone who sells tapes and CD's from their home or the trunk of their car? It's a form of entrepreneurship. Do you know someone who sells cakes or pies during holiday times? Or hand-crafted items at Christmas time? They are all forms of entrepreneurship. The first point to remember is no matter how small a venture it is, if it makes money for you, it's a business and the business is entrepreneurship. No matter what career you finally choose, it is important that the idea of entrepreneurship be a part of the foundation of your thinking. That is, taking what you have and making it work for you but always **LEGALLY.** It means being a **SELF-STARTER**, creative and innovative it means training yourself to always see the potential in a thing or situation. Historically, from the poorest to the richest communities, entrepreneurship has played a significant role in maintaining every society. As a matter of fact, if you research, you will find that many multi-millionaires began with just ___AN IDEA___, a plan and an aptitude for hard work. Of course, if in the next few years you decide to explore the world of entrepreneurship as a career goal, you will want to attend a business college or get some other formal training that includes the various aspects of business from creating a business plan, to financial and time management to forecasting and global marketing and beyond. It's your world and the sky is the limit! In the meantime, as long as the spirit of entrepreneurship is a part of your thinking, you will always be able to survive and achieve no matter what career you choose.

Love Always

DAY 31 JOURNAL

_____

_____

_____

_____

_____

_____

_____

_____

_____

_____

_____

_____

_____

_____

_____

_____

_____

_____

_____

_____

_____

_____

_____

"Goals that are not written down are Just wishes."

-Anonymous

PART TWO

All About Goals

STOP!

Please read this important information on goal setting

First, let's ask ourselves the question, what are goals? According to Webster's dictionary, a goal is "something that you are trying to do or achieve." Do you want to succeed in your studies, in athletics, or in any of the many other areas of your life? Of course you do! Goal setting is a major key. The President of the United States does it. CEO's of large corporations do it. Elementary, Middle and High School principals do it. Most people who are successful in life practice goal setting. Why? The number one reason why you should set goals is because goals serve as a blue print or road map to where you want to go as a teen or as an adult. Just as there are maps to navigate one's traveling, your goals sheets (on the following pages) will serve the same purpose. The number two reason why you should set goals is so that you can be specific and clear about where you are going. Once you begin your goal setting program, watch out for setbacks. One of the principle ingredients to have in place to help avoid setbacks is **accountability**. Nothing in this world is 100%.

However, if you want to avoid simple pit falls and unnecessary road blocks, **find a partner, someone you can be accountable to.** Your *"accountability partner"* can be a parent, a teacher, a coach, a mentor or any other adult that you trust and who you know wants to see you succeed. Make a date with your accountability partner and discuss with them how you plan to proceed and ask for their suggestions, comments and concerns. Take notes at each meeting. Have them sign off on your beginning plan. Set up a schedule to meet with your partner for thirty minutes each week to discuss your progress. It will be their job to sign off on the bottom of your Goals Sheet each marking period, agreeing that you will meet your goals for that particular marking period. When the going gets tough, and you get discouraged, tired, lazy TALK TO YOUR ACCOUNTABILITY PARTNER. Once you have had your initial meeting with your accountability partner decide specifically what it is you want to accomplish. Then plan and take one small step at a time to make it happen. Each step leads you to the next step and you continue the process until you are at the top or at least where you want to go.

The goals sections found in this book have been designed to assist you each marking period in establishing goals and then, by taking one small step at a time, achieving them. In setting your goals, try not to generalize. For example, you might say, "I want better grades next marking period." A stronger, more helpful goal to set would be, *"I plan to move from a "D" to a "B" by the end of the marking period."* Instead of saying, "I plan to lose some weight by the end of the marking period," say **"I will lose 10 lbs. by the end of the marking period."** Remember, small steps are better. Working with your accountability partner and using the goals sheets found in this book, each marking period you will decide exactly what it is you want to achieve and the steps you plan to take to succeed. Remember, small changes can make a big difference and there's no such thing as failure. I like to call them second chances and sometimes we can all use a second chance. So, don't beat yourself up if you just "come close." You still have the next marking period to improve. **SO STICK TO IT! The victory will be sweet.** There's an old tried and true adage that works here. "If at first you don't succeed, try, try again." Challenge yourself to do better.

You don't have to push yourself to the limit all the time but you should want to move closer to your goals each marking period. One size does not fit all. You are you so make your goals with that in mind. Your ATTITUDE will play a big part in whether you win or lose. A quote that I personally love is, _"It is the attitude that you have toward yourself that will determine your attitude toward your world."_ Now, every small step you take, large or small, **CELEBRATE!** Do something nice for yourself and look forward to achieving your next goal. Most importantly, **HAVE FUN!** SO, **ON YOUR MARK, GET SET, GO!** From the mouth of Zig Ziglar...

**"SEE YOU AT THE TOP!"**

FIRST SCHOOL YEAR
20_____20_____

FIRST MARKING PERIOD

GOAL #1_____

_____

STEP #3_____

_____

STEP #2_____

_____

STEP #1_____

_____

GOAL #2_____

_____

STEP #3_____

_____

STEP #2_____

_____

STEP #1_____

Accountability Partner Signature:_____

SECOND MARKING PERIOD

GOAL #1_____

_____

STEP #3_____

_____

STEP #2_____

_____

STEP #1_____

_____

GOAL #2_____

_____

STEP #3_____

_____

STEP #2_____

_____

STEP #1_____

Accountability Partner Signature:_____

THIRD MARKING PERIOD

GOAL #1_____

_____

STEP #3_____

_____

STEP #2_____

_____

STEP #1_____

_____

GOAL #2_____

_____

STEP #3_____

_____

STEP #2_____

_____

STEP #1_____

Accountability Partner Signature:_____

FOURTH MARKING PERIOD

GOAL #1_____

_____

STEP #3_____

_____

STEP #2_____

_____

STEP #1_____

_____

GOAL #2_____

_____

STEP #3_____

_____

STEP #2_____

_____

STEP #1_____

Accountability Partner Signature:_____

SECOND SCHOOL YEAR
20_____20_____

FIRST MARKING PERIOD

GOAL #1_____

_____

STEP #3_____

_____

STEP #2_____

_____

STEP #1_____

_____

GOAL #2_____

_____

STEP #3_____

_____

STEP #2_____

_____

STEP #1_____

Accountability Partner Signature:_____

SECOND MARKING PERIOD

GOAL #1_____

_____

STEP #3_____

_____

STEP #2_____

_____

STEP #1_____

_____

GOAL #2_____

_____

STEP #3_____

_____

STEP #2_____

_____

STEP #1_____

_____

Accountability Partner Signature:_____

THIRD MARKING PERIOD

GOAL #1_____
_____

STEP #3_____
_____

STEP #2_____
_____

STEP #1_____
_____

GOAL #2_____
_____

STEP #3_____
_____

STEP #2_____
_____

STEP #1_____
_____

Accountability Partner Signature:_____

FOURTH MARKING PERIOD

GOAL #1_____

_____

STEP #3_____

_____

STEP #2_____

_____

STEP #1_____

_____

GOAL #2_____

_____

STEP #3_____

_____

STEP #2_____

_____

STEP #1_____

_____

Accountability Partner Signature:_____

THIRD SCHOOL YEAR
20_____20_____

FIRST MARKING PERIOD

GOAL #1_____

_____

STEP #3_____

_____

STEP #2_____

_____

STEP #1_____

_____

GOAL #2_____

_____

STEP #3_____

_____

STEP #2_____

_____

STEP #1_____

Accountability Partner Signature:_____

SECOND MARKING PERIOD

GOAL #1_____

_____

STEP #3_____

_____

STEP #2_____

_____

STEP #1_____

_____

GOAL #2_____

_____

STEP #3_____

_____

STEP #2_____

_____

STEP #1_____

Accountability Partner Signature:_____

THIRD MARKING PERIOD

GOAL #1_____

_____

STEP #3_____

_____

STEP #2_____

_____

STEP #1_____

_____

GOAL #2_____

_____

STEP #3_____

_____

STEP #2_____

_____

STEP #1_____

Accountability Partner Signature:_____

FOURTH MARKING PERIOD

GOAL #1_____

_____

STEP #3_____

_____

STEP #2_____

_____

STEP #1_____

_____

GOAL #2_____

_____

STEP #3_____

_____

STEP #2_____

_____

STEP #1_____

Accountability Partner Signature:_____

Order & Contact Information

<u>ORDER NOW!</u>

Amazon.Com/BluZipper Books

<u>Email</u>

bluzipper@gmail.com

<u>SOCIAL MEDIA</u>

All Social Media@/bluzipper media

ABOUT THE EDITOR

Margaret Ford-Taylor is a nationally acclaimed writer, director, actress and arts administrator.

Among many critically recognized acting awards and commendations, she received her first Emmy nomination for her performance in the public television production, "American Women: Echoes and Dreams." Her last film appearance was as Aunt Edy in Denzel Washington's Antwon Fisher.

Author of more than 40 critically acknowledged and nationally produced stage works, Miss Ford-Taylor's second Emmy nomination was as the writer of the ABC television documentary, "The Second Reconstruction."

She was affiliated with the world-renown Karamu Performing Arts Center of Cleveland, Ohio for more than 30 years, serving as its Executive Director for ten.

She has taught on the faculties of Kent State University and Akron University, retiring from the Dramatic Arts Faculty of Cleveland State University in 2008. As a teacher and mentor many of her students are recognized among the list of noted professionals in the performing arts field and other industries.

About The Co-Author

As far back as I can remember I have been interested in entrepreneurship. It all started when I was a paper boy with the Cleveland Press News-Paper. At 11 years of age I won a contest for signing up new customers. After a long afternoon of delivering papers I was approached by some guys I knew from my neighborhood. They said "Hey, paper boy, you want to make some real money, you need to come hang with us" All the while they were laughing. A short time after that, I join their gang on the Eastside of Cleveland and begin my introduction to experimenting with drugs and alcohol. I didn't realize it then but I had just enrolled into "side-walk University" to major in *"street-sense."*

I am amazed at how far *"street sense"* can take you…Unfortunately, that's exactly where it will also leave you. That is also where I begin a career of always trying to gain an upper hand on any and every situation. After a few years with that bunch I wanted out. I thought I had escaped with only the small scar under my bottom lip where I received stitches from being hit and kicked because I made a decision to leave a life of negativity and begin living more positively. Unfortunately, the beginning stages of alcohol and drug abuse along with an extreme case of emotional immaturity were present as well.

Hence, there were a number of detours. Once, during one detour, I was over 800 miles away from home, addicted, homeless twice, with the possibility of federal prison looming over my head; that was coupled with strong feelings of guilt, shame, and remorse. I begin to realize that I had just squandered one of the most precious years of my life…**My YOUTH**. As an adult I tried on several occasion to gain those years back, but to no avail and that was a troubling reality that I had to accept. Somehow, I eventually managed to navigate my way through high school, graduating on the merit roll and with perfect attendance. I always had a strong thirst for knowledge. So I'm not surprised that today I work around educators, who I BELIEVE are some of the brightest and talented in their field (Mary M. Bethune School 2011-2012). But back then, I was still clue less. One day, through divine intervention, I decided I had had enough and I made up my mind to throw in the towel. I was FORTUNATE. With some good counseling and willing workers I BEGAN the journey of rebuilding my life mentally, physically, emotionally, and spiritually all *"one day at a time."*

However, when I juxtapose to where I am today it's no comparison. I am extremely grateful. Currently, I reside in University Circle in the great *"comeback"* City, Cleveland, Ohio. In January 2012 the notable Forbes Magazine voted University Circle as one of the 10-prettiest neighborhoods In America. Presently, I work not far from where I live at a

 Pre-K-8 school where I am a Paraprofessional (a really cool name for an assistant teacher). I work with children with special needs. My current assignment is a one-on-one with an 11-year-old student name Trevon who has autism. (Relax everyone. His parents approved of me using his name). Trevon doesn't communicate very well. He repeats everything. It's called **"echolalia."** Trevon is special to me. In his own way, he's taught me so much. So I pause at this time in my life to give a brief shout out to my little buddy. Trevon has a gentle spirit. He is extremely funny, a sharp dresser in and out of school uniform and a lover of all kinds of music, especially the BLUES, and an all-around joy to work with.

With no hesitation I will say working with Trevon has been one of the highlights and best experiences of my ENTIRE adult working career. Let me pause to say, if you have special needs students in your life; treat them with love, respect, and genuine kindness. YOU'LL be the winner and God will bless your life for that. Finally, my hope is that this book will inspire someone to follow their dreams and never let them die. I close with one of my favorite sayings from the scriptures, *"the race is not given to the swift nor to the strong but to those who endure to...THE END!"*

ACKNOWLEDGEMENTS

First and foremost, **I MUST** thank God for His ***"AMAZING GRACE!"***

-Your Son, Michael Kenneth Chapman!

To Mom and Willie: Thanks for the Thursday steak dinners–and I do mean every Thursday, **[unless my "big brother George" or my first cousin Tiffany Moore beat me to it]** smile. Thanks for LIFE!

-Your Son, Michael!

To my immediate family: ***My*** Aunt Gloria Moore, my big brother George D. Chapman, my two older sisters Debra M. Chapman and Nadine M. Chapman, all my $1^{st}, 2^{nd}, 3^{rd}$, and 4th, cousins and all my nieces and nephews. Thank you all for listening to me **EVERY** Thanksgiving about Every wild and crazy idea I have ever brought to the dinner table, most importantly, thank you all for not laughing at me…Well, at least not in my face–thank you guys and I Love you all!   -Michael!

To Miss Margaret Ford-Taylor: You are more than just a great editor, writer, actress and acting coach you are truly a great friend. You are an author's dream and your gift will be a blessing to many young women around the world…Thanks for your support, wisdom and expertise…May God continue to bless your life and your family.   -'My' Michael!

To my man of God and first lady: Dr. R. A. Vernon and first Lady Vernon: I thank you both for speaking into my life since April 11, 2004 (Easter Sunday) and for always *"N-COURAGING"* me to go to the next level in ALL areas of my life.   -Brother Chapman!

To my son, Quameen *"Q"* Vernon: You will be a strong leader in your chosen field and I will continue to tell you that until I see it manifested. You have charisma and people like you for you. Always follow your heart, but make sure you finish your master's program! God bless you!

-Love always, Dad!

To my beautiful God–daughter, Mariah **"Precious"** Weaver: God has an AWESOME plan for your life and I will live to see it come to pass. I truly appreciate you being in my life…With all my heart I love you very much! By the way, have you read your **"One-Year-Bible"** today?

-Love always, Your God-Father!

To the 31-letter writers: This book would have **ALL** blank pages had it not been for you all. May God continue to bless **ALL** of you and your families.

-Michael K. Chapman

Made in United States
North Haven, CT
02 September 2022

23569839R00096